D1175890

MARQUETTE
AND
JOLIET

Voyagers on the Mississippi

MARQUETTE AND JOLIET

by Ronald Syme

illustrated by William Stobbs
William Morrow and Company
New York 1974

Library of Congress Cataloging in Publication Data

Syme, Ronald (date)
    Marquette and Joliet: voyagers on the Mississippi.

    SUMMARY: A biography of the two seventeenth-century French explorers who were the first to chart the course of the Mississippi River.
    1. Marquette, Jacques, 1637-1675—Juvenile literature. 2. Joliet, Louis, 1645-1700—Juvenile literature. 3. Mississippi River—Discovery and exploration—Juvenile literature. [1. Marquette, Jacques, 1637-1675. 2. Joliet, Louis, 1645-1700. 3. Mississippi River—Discovery and exploration. 4. Explorers, French] I. Stobbs, William, illus. II. Title
F352.S95 1974   977'.01'0922 [B] [920]   73-14504
ISBN 0-688-20105-9
ISBN 0-688-30105-3 (lib. bdg.)

The little agricultural town of Laon lay in
the heart of that part of the rich French
countryside named Picardy. From there to
Paris was eighty miles in a southwesterly
direction. White-walled houses with red-
tiled, crooked roofs lined the cobbled main
street. In the little market square near one
end of that street was a fragrant-scented
bakery, a cobbler's shop, and a dark, dusty
little general store, smelling strongly of new

5

rope and leather, where the local farmers could buy their simple tools.

The menfolk of the town and the nearby farms were short, sturdy, weather-beaten fellows whose wiry strength and sharpness of eye had earned for them the reputation of being the finest archers in the whole of France. In earlier times they had fought the English at the great battles of Agincourt and Crécy. Those battles took place on their native soil of Picardy.

They were a people who believed strongly in tradition. For this reason, they preferred their own leaders to the best officers that the splendid army of France could provide. The Marquette family of Laon had supplied many such leaders during the past two or three hundred years. They lived and fought and sometimes died in the company of their own sturdy bowmen of Picardy.

In the early 1600's, two hundred years

after the battle of Agincourt, the Marquette family still flourished. They owned a solid, gray-walled, steeply roofed house down near the market square. Less than a mile outside the town lay the rich green fields and sheltering belts of timber that comprised their three extensive farms.

Jacques Lespérance Marquette was born in 1637. As he grew older, the townspeople began to notice a difference between him and the rest of his family. The Marquettes always had been short, wide-shouldered, and light-haired. They had good, square faces, gray or blue eyes, and unusually fair complexions. Young Jacques Marquette was tall, slender, and black-haired. There was little of the robust countryman in his appearance.

"His mother's blood has proved the stronger," declared the older folk. Marie Quintal, as she was before her marriage to

the boy's father, came from the province
of Gascony far to the southwest. She was
dark, like most of the Gascons and the boy
seemed to have taken after her.

The good people of Laon began to see
other differences when Jacques Marquette
was in his early teens. The Marquette family had never been great scholars; they
scraped through the village school, learned
arithmetic up to long division, and forgot

about higher education. Still, they picked up enough to run their prosperous farms, for they were wise in the ways of soil and weather and livestock.

In contrast, Jacques Marquette passed through the village school and, without pausing, began to attend the Catholic seminary, a few miles outside the little town. Selected young students were trained there to become Roman Catholic priests. Jacques' younger brother, Jules, followed more traditional Marquette custom. He was plodding sturdily through junior grades at the village school and already taking an active part in the management of the farms. In appearance he was a true Marquette: short, square-shouldered, and fair-haired.

"It's Jules who'll get the farms," prophesied the neighbors. They felt that Jacques was cut out to be a scholar and that he never would make a farmer.

The people of Laon did not know, however, that Jacques Marquette was more adventurous than any of his family. When he reached his early teens, his imagination was stirred by the tales the priests had told him of Jesuit missionaries in far-off New France, as the French settlements along the Saint Lawrence River then were called. He heard how those fanatical, obstinate, and gallant men lived and worked in the interior of the vast, inhospitable, and little-known country. The missionaries traveled great distances by canoe or on foot, developed the endurance to live in primitive huts among barbaric Indian tribes, and frequently met death at the hands of the savages whom they tried to convert. They led a thankless, disappointing existence in which they were sustained by their unshakeable faith in the cause of Christianity.

"They are great men no doubt," said

Jacques' father, when they discussed the Jesuit missionaries one day. "I myself think — though I would not like our priests to hear of it — that they are too good to spend their lives trying to teach Christianity to ungrateful savages. They would be better advised to devote their saintly labors to the poorest classes in France, where they'd find a higher reward."

Still, Jacques had made up his mind to enter the Order of Jesus, the religious fraternity to which the Jesuits belonged, but the time had not come yet to reveal his decision. He did so just after his seventeenth birthday.

"It is true that the Order toils for the sake of Christianity," Jacques told his disappointed father, "but it seems that their outlook is changing. During the past few years the reports of their missionaries in New France contain news and theories of geography. They write about the courses of un-explored rivers, the direction of winds, and the supposed deposits of minerals such as copper. Perhaps in earlier years the Order's missionaries were too narrow in their out-look, but nowadays they are carrying out valuable work of exploration in addition to their religious duties. While my ambition is to help bring Christianity to the Indian tribes, I also would like to discover some great unknown lake or map the width of some unknown region."

"I would have preferred your help mark-ing the boundaries of those few acres I am planning to buy," his father replied shortly. "It's land that can be made to produce good crops. I hope you change your mind."

Jacques Marquette had a share of his family's obstinacy. He did not change his mind. When he was still only seventeen years old, he left his solid and prosperous family home. He never returned to it, and Jules was the one who inherited the farms, exactly as the neighbors had predicted.

For the next twelve years Jacques worked and studied at the Jesuit College in Paris. In 1666, at the age of twenty-nine, he sailed for New France as Father Marquette of the Order of Jesus. This decisive step was destined to place his name in the pages of American history.

When Jacques Marquette was already eight years old, another boy was born in 1645 more than 3000 miles away in the French settlement of Quebec. His name was Louis Joliet, and he was the son of a successful wagonmaker and boatbuilder.

Like Marquette, young Joliet was attracted to the Catholic faith. As he grew older, he attended the Jesuit seminary in Quebec. At the age of seventeen, he, too, confronted an irate father and informed him that he had chosen to follow a different life; he had decided to become a Jesuit missionary.

Joliet was accepted by the Order and began his training as a priest. At that point the lives of the two young men began to converge. Jacques Marquette in Paris continued to study for the priesthood. Louis Joliet, increasingly attracted by the love of the wilderness that influenced so many young Frenchmen, lasted for only two years at the seminary. At the end of that time he decided to resign.

His decision was a surprise. Joliet was a placid, steady-going, and rather unimaginative young man, not the kind to make sudden alterations in his plans for the future.

"I have decided," he explained to the Abbé Laval, "that I do not have a true love of missionary work. The real attraction for

me was that so many of the Fathers labor
in the wilds far from civilized outposts.
From the little I know about the Indians,
I have begun to believe that their tribal way
of life in the forests and on the prairies has
a greater hold on them than the teachings
of Christianity ever will be able to obtain.
Even I, a Frenchman, find myself envious
at times of the liberty and independence of
the Indians."

"You are an honest young man, and I will tell you that you are not alone in your doubts," replied the Abbé. "Yet the work of our Order must continue. What career do you intend to follow, my son?"

"I hope to become a fur trader," Joliet replied. "Apart from a skill with a carpenter's tools, fur trading is the only work I know anything about."

Louis Joliet left the Jesuits and disappeared into the vast tracts of forest and the sunlit meadows around the Great Lakes. The Jesuits had provided him with a good education and taught him to use a compass and to make accurate charts. During the next few years he lived close to the Indians, learned their languages, and studied their ways. He made a point of keeping faith with them, and gradually the Indians grew to understand that Joliet was honest.

By the time he was twenty-three, the government officials in Quebec had become familiar with his name. His life and ways were very similar to those of the hundreds of other young Frenchmen who had run off into the woods to fight and live with their Indian companions. But the administrators looked upon Joliet as a trustworthy young man who could write very clear reports. Some of the maps that he had supplied at their request were excellent. The officials allowed Joliet to carry on as a fur trader at a time when the trade was a strict monopoly jealously preserved by the government and by the few men to whom licenses were issued. In return, Joliet acted as a kind of scout, intelligence agent, and part-time explorer on their behalf.

The governor of New France in Joliet's day was a titled French aristocrat named the Sieur de Courcelles. His second in command, or intendant, was a hard and capable sixty-two-year-old man named Jean Baptiste Talon. He was one of the best administrators that France ever sent to the New World.

Reports of copper deposits near Lake Superior had reached Talon from Jesuit missionaries and wandering Frenchmen. The intendant was interested in the production of this ore for export to France. He invited Joliet to undertake a journey to Lake Superior and report as to whether the copper could be brought to Quebec by some route better than that of the Ottawa River, which had a number of difficult portages. Joliet set off on this trip in 1668.

By then Marquette had been in New France for two years. After spending some months at Quebec in order to accustom himself to the new way of life, he set off with a companion named Father Dablon for Saint Mary's River between Lake Superior

18

and Lake Huron. At the foot of the wide rapids of Sault Sainte Marie they built their mission, the earliest in what is now the State of Michigan. Far to the west of them, Joliet was cruising in his canoe along the northern shore of Lake Superior. The young explorer gradually was finding out that the copper deposits were not sufficient for development.

Thirty-one year-old Marquette appeared to like his hard and cheerless existence among the Indians. He agreed with Father Dablon, who wrote:

> The country in this region resembles an earthly paradise. But the way to it is as hard to find as the path to heaven.

Only men of great faith could have found any resemblance to paradise in the way those two Fathers were compelled to live.

19

Even wandering fur traders would have grumbled at such primitive conditions. Marquette wrote cheerfully of the bark hut their Indian assistants helped them to build at Sault Sainte Marie. It was ventilated by numberless crevices in the thin walls. The interior of the hut always smelled of smoke, and when the wind was in the wrong direction, it became so filled with this smoke that the missionaries, choking and coughing, had to stumble outside. The food consisted of sagamite, or pounded Indian corn mixed with scraps of fish. There was pumpkin baked in the ashes of a fire and sometimes whitefish, which Father Marquette, remembering his boyhood in Laon, netted in the nearby river.

Marquette wrote:

By day we read and studied by the light that streamed in through the hole in the roof

that served as a chimney. At night, by the blaze of our fire. The only candles we had were those we used for our altar.

Marquette also noted that he and Dablon rose from the sheets of bark on which they slept — covered with a single blanket — at four o'clock in the morning. At eight o'clock they opened their door to the Indians.

As many of these proved great nuisances, we took the liberty of turning out the most tiresome and undisciplined, an action which few of them ever resented. With the others, we sometimes sat by the fire and smoked our pipes.

While he was becoming used to this thankless way of life, Marquette's enthusiasm remained high. Endless questions about this little-known country passed through his mind. How far was it to the Western Sea as the Pacific Ocean then was called? Did any great rivers run westward across the continent and eventually flow into that sea? What about the other great river that the Indians called the Mississippi? Did it flow in a southwesterly direction until it reached the Western Sea, or did it flow southward to the warm blue waters of the Gulf of Mexico?

After spending a year at Sault Sainte Marie, Marquette left to go to the western end of Lake Superior. At a place called La Pointe in those days — the modern Wisconsin town of Ashland — he founded another mission of his own. His Indian congregation were Hurons and Ottawas who had fled westward to escape attacking Iroquois. Yet before the unfortunate refugees had spent much time beside Lake Superior they discovered to their sorrow that they were

exposed to the almost equally dangerous Sioux of the Western plains. To try to instruct these Indians, while they were constantly glancing over their shoulders for fear of an enemy, was a hopeless task for Marquette. Terror so filled their minds that there was little attention left in them for the teachings of Christianity.

Among Marquette's Indians were a few members of the Illinois tribe. They were not refugees like the others and were more interesting people.

"Our river flows southward to join another even greater river," said the Illinois. "We have heard that it rolls on southward to flow through a country much warmer than this. The Indians who live there plant two crops of corn every year. Beyond that tribe live other people who wear glass beads and are said to have seen large canoes with sails at the mouth of the great river."

Glass beads meant that those far-off Indians were in touch with Europeans. But had those "large canoes with sails" been seen on the Gulf of Mexico or the Western Sea? This fascinating question remained unanswered in Marquette's mind. It caused his interest in exploration to rise even higher. He wrote in his journal:

If I can get the canoe which the Illinois

have promised to make for me, I intend —
with some other Frenchmen who can speak
with these tribes in their own tongue — to
navigate this river and reach those unknown
tribes. I then will be able to decide the question of the true direction in which the great
river flows.

Marquette must have thought that there
was little chance of his ever being able to
make that great voyage. Few other Frenchmen ever came to La Pointe. He had no
supplies of his own, practically no money,
and no equipment. There must have been
times when Father Marquette envied the
coureurs de bois and the French fur traders
who, equipped with canoes, muskets, and
adequate supplies, moved fearlessly for
hundreds of miles across the Great Lakes
or penetrated forest-lined rivers.

More urgent matters soon put these
thoughts out of his mind. The Huron and

Ottawa Indians decided to leave La Pointe and return eastward. This time they chose to settle at Michilimackinac, only a few miles away from his old mission at Sault Sainte Marie. Once again Marquette and his helpers set about building rickety and smoke-filled mission huts. In addition, he persuaded the Indians to erect several spare cabins that could be used to accommodate any fresh refugees.

As gray skies and increasingly piercing winds announced the approach of the winter of 1672, two lonely canoes paddled to the shore overlooked by Marquette's mission. Out stepped a husky, fur-clad young Frenchman. Behind him came five other Frenchmen, whom Marquette recognized as *voyageurs,* or professional rivermen, by their heavy bodies and arms, their clay pipes and red, knitted woolen caps. When these strangers had unloaded their canoes

and carried them above the water's edge, their leader approached Marquette.

"I am Louis Joliet," he said. "I have heard a great deal of you, Father, and of your interest in exploration. We have plenty of provisions and equipment. May I ask that we be allowed to remain here until the return of spring? We are now too late to return to Quebec before the arrival of ice."

"You, too, I have heard of," replied Marquette. "Indeed, I have used your maps from time to time. You are a most welcome guest at my mission, and you may remain here with pleasure."

Marquette spoke with sincerity. He was delighted with the thought of having civilized companions with whom to share the long, dark, and silent months that lay ahead. He indeed had heard of Joliet's roaming expeditions; perhaps he was even a little envious of the roving life led by this venturesome young fellow-countryman.

During the weeks and months that followed, Marquette's existence became more comfortable. With skilled hands the *voyageurs* strengthened his hut against the freezing winds. They procured fresh meat in generous quantities, carved simple articles of furniture, and quickly established friendly terms with the Indians at the mission.

Marquette and Joliet soon grew to enjoy each other's company. They spent their evenings beside a blazing log fire, smoking their pipes and comparing their experiences. Before long Joliet was discussing his plans of exploration for the following spring.

"The Intendant, Monsieur Talon, is pressing me to find some tributary of the Mississippi River," he said. "Then he wants me to descend it until I reach the big river itself. I am expected to go as far as I can and try to discover what sea it reaches. Monsieur Talon has treated me well in the past; I will probably undertake the journey, although it will bring me no direct profit."

"Then you do not believe the Indian reports of the great monsters and the deadly heat and the vast whirlpools that are said to be found along the lower reaches of that river?" asked Marquette.

Joliet shrugged his shoulders. "No more than you do, Father," he replied. "As I have told you, I attended the Jesuit seminary in Quebec during my younger days. I know that the missionaries of your Order are taught to ignore such fabulous tales. It is good teaching; I myself have followed it during my travels."

Marquette remained silent for a while. "This journey of yours is one that I have sometimes dreamed of making myself," he said presently. "I had the selfish ambition, unworthy of the Order to which I belong, of wanting to be the first European to discover the true course of the Mississippi. But there were many reasons why I could never make it. You, my friend, are aware of them. I doubt that our Father Superior in Quebec would look kindly on my request to set off on a voyage of exploration. We are supposed only to report on what we learn during our travels that will help to bring Christianity to the Indians."

"Why not find out for sure what the Father Superior thinks?" asked Joliet. "In another year or so any such application from a Jesuit probably will be refused, if not by his Order then by the administration in Quebec. Just before I left that settlement in the spring of this year, the new governor, Count Frontenac, began to indicate that he dislikes the Jesuits just as much as he dislikes Intendant Talon. I think that Count Frontenac is more interested in dealing with the Iroquois than he is in any future plans of exploration. No one can blame him. The harder he hits the Iroquois, the better off we all will be. But warfare is a more familiar thing to him than the exploration of unknown rivers, especially exploration by Jesuit missionaries."

Marquette thought this information over for a few moments. Most of what Joliet had told him was entirely new. "I think I already may be too late," he said. "In view of what you say, I will have to put all thoughts of exploration out of my mind."

"I did not advise that, Father," said Joliet. "I said that you should delay no longer. Make your application now. If you receive permission, you can accompany us. We have room for you in our canoes."

34

"You may be right," said Marquette with sudden hope. "Perhaps on our way down the river we could meet tribes among whom our missionaries might establish themselves. I myself long have wanted to build a mission among the Illinois people. If I came with you, I perhaps could be of some slight service, for I speak six Indian languages and am known already to the Illinois tribe."

"Then let me carry your application to Quebec," Joliet suggested. "There are certain things I have to do in the settlements before I set out on another long voyage. I must see the intendant as soon as possible, and two of my *voyageurs* are anxious to return to their homes in Montreal. I must get new men to replace them."

The long winter ended, and the melting snow began to drip from the dark eaves of the cabins. Joliet and his two *voyageurs* departed in a single canoe. As Marquette stood on the bank and watched the little craft vanish downstream into the early-morning mist, he prayed that the Reverend Father would see fit to grant his humble application.

Joliet and his hardy *voyageurs* traveled swiftly and tirelessly across fog-bound lakes and flooded rivers. Before the fresh green-ery of the trees had begun to darken into maturity, they arrived back from their 2000-mile voyage. On May 9, 1673, Marquette received the necessary permission to make the trip.

On May 17, Marquette, Joliet, and five *voyageurs* set off from the mission. The Huron and Ottawa Indians were left at the place to tend their growing crops and — as Father Marquette hoped — to continue to practice the rites of the Catholic Church in which he had instructed them.

They paddled southward for the first two

days and then swung onto a westerly course toward Lake Michigan. As they passed along the northern shore of that lake they made for the land at the close of each day. Between the edge of the lake and the nearby verge of the forest they built their campfire, quickly erected a leafy shelter if the sky was overcast and threatening, and roamed along the shore with their muskets to procure fresh meat. As a missionary, Marquette was forbidden to bear arms, but there were plenty of other daily tasks awaiting him. Wearing his somber black soutane, or cassock, he busied himself around the camp, helped with the canoes, often cooked the meals, and sometimes cast the fishing net with which he was most skillful. Sitting beside the fire in the twilight, he carefully wrote the events of the day into his journal. Joliet also kept his own daily record of the voyage.

ROUTE OF MARQUETTE-JOLIET DISCOVERY
OF MISSISSIPPI RIVER IN 1673
Present-day place names appear in brackets.

NEW FRANCE

Quebec

St. Lawrence R.

Ottawa R.

Montreal

Lachine Rapids

L. Superior

Sault
Ste. Marie

La Pointe
[Ashland]

Michilimackinac

L. Huron

Wisconsin R.

[Green
Bay]

Minneapolis]

L. Winnebago

L. Ontario

[Prairie du Chien]

L. Michigan

L. Erie

[Milwaukee]

Mississippi R.

Illinois R.

[Chicago]

Missouri R.

Ohio R.

[Kansas City]

[St. Louis]

Appalachian Mts.

Atlantic Ocean

Arkansas R.

[Greenville]

Mississippi R.

[Biloxi]

[Baton Rouge]

[New Orleans]

Mississippi Delta

Gulf o f M e x i c o

0   100   200   300   Miles

Joliet, a sturdy figure in leather shirt and tasseled leggings, led his two canoes into Grande Baie on the western coast of Lake Michigan. (English settlers later changed this name to Green Bay.) There they came to a camp of the Folle Avoine, or Wild Oats Indians, as the Menominee tribe was known in those times.

Marquette wrote:

> The wild oat is a sort of grass that grows naturally in the small rivers with muddy bottoms and in swampy places. It greatly resembles the wild oats that grow amid our wheat. The ears grow upon hollow stems. They emerge from the water about the month of June and continue growing until they rise about two feet above it.

Marquette had the love of fresh knowledge and the eye for detail that made the Jesuit missionaries such reliable explorers.

He carefully described how the Indians
went in their canoes at the end of the summer and shook the growing rice so that the
grains fell into their canoes. They then
dried the oats and "put them in a skin
made into a bag, thrust it into a hole, and
trod it with their feet so that the grain sep-
arated from the straw and was easily win-
nowed."

These friendly Indians did their best to

discourage Marquette and Joliet from their voyage down the Mississippi River. According to them, the banks were inhabited by tribes "who never show any mercy to strangers, but break their heads without any cause." They went on to retell the familiar stories about the river with which Joliet and Marquette were already familiar.

They also said that the great river was very dangerous, when one does not know the difficult places, that it was full of horrible monsters which devoured men and canoes together; that there was even a demon who was heard from a great distance, who barred the way and swallowed up all who ventured to approach; finally that the heat was so excessive in those countries that it would inevitably cause our death.

The five *voyageurs,* who spoke only a slight smattering of the Ottawa Indian language, sat stolidly and smoked their pipes while all these fearsome tales were being re-counted by the native speakers. Joliet did not interpret what was being said. He knew his *voyageurs* and realized that the highly superstitious men were not looking forward greatly to this voyage down a large and un-known river. Probably they would be brought to mutiny if they heard of the supposed dangers that awaited them.

"They are good and simple fellows," he said to Marquette, "who expect little except ample food for their stomachs, money in their pockets with which to buy ribbons and laces for their sweethearts in Montreal, and plenty of strong tobacco for their pipes. It is best to leave their imaginations un-troubled."

The little expedition passed on through Green Bay and arrived at the mouth of the Fox River, which flowed into the southern end. Soaked to the waist and buffeted by the cold, rushing water, they dragged their canoes up the long rapids. Then they launched themselves on the more tranquil waters of pretty little Lake Winnebago and paddled along it until they reached the southern shore. Maskouten Indians guided them along a two-mile portage over the prairies and through a swamp to the waters of the Wisconsin River. "Having brought us thus far, these kindly Indians returned home, leaving us alone in this unknown country in the hands of Providence." (A monument was erected to Marquette in 1895 on the Fox-Wisconsin portage.)

Once again the explorers climbed aboard their frail canoes and pushed off from the shore. They knew that now they were embarked fully on their great voyage.

On either hand stretched the endless expanse of the green prairie, darkened here and there with pleasant groves of trees or grazing herds of elk and deer. The river shone peacefully in the sun, and a cool breeze dissolved the slight ripples on the water caused by the onward progress of the gliding canoes. The scenery was so attractive and the surroundings so pleasant that the silent moodiness of the *voyageurs* — who never appreciated strange rivers — began to vanish.

"It is not a countryside that one would imagine to be haunted by demons," a man named Jacques remarked presently. "That, from the little I understood, is what those Indians were warning us of. For myself, I always have believed that evil spirits are found among dark crags, gloomy pine forests, and violent rivers racing between black walls of rock. This present stretch of country is fairer than any I have seen in New France, and the sun shines more warmly than in our northern land."

The spirits of the Frenchmen continued to rise throughout the day. As the sun neared the western horizon, they paddled to the shore, unloaded their canoes, turned the light craft upside down, and kindled a fire. For their evening meal they ate steaks of the deer that Joliet had shot soon after they landed. Later the little party sat round the warm glow of their fire, smoking their pipes and lazily discussing the events of the day. With a single blanket to cover each of them, the men slept peacefully.

The next day, and the day after it, were spent in passing undisturbed along the southward course of this lazy, friendly, and beautiful river. Rich lands stretched on either side. Islands situated in midstream were covered with dense groves of walnut and oak, their massive branches festooned with gracefully drooping wreaths of grapevine. Here and there they caught sight of

grazing "Illinois oxen clothed in wool," or the buffalo, which the French had learned to recognize during the past twenty or so years. The voyage was as pleasant a one as the canoe men ever had experienced, their only worry being caused by the sandbars that sometimes appeared in midstream. The sun continued to shine with unusual warmth so that the *voyageurs* were prompted to remove their heavy woolen shirts and to cool their sweating faces in the crystal clear water.

Marquette named this stream the Mesconsing, for it was thus, he believed, that the Indians pronounced it. A later French missionary named Hennepin wrote the name as Ouisconsin, and when New France had become but a memory, English settlers came to pronounce the name as Wisconsin.

This delightful period of the voyage ended on June 17. On that day they saw on their right an expanse of wide, low-lying fields bounded in the distance by a line of rugged hills. (The town of Prairie du Chien stands there today.) Beyond the slender bows of their canoes the Frenchmen saw a deeper, mightier stream sweeping across their present course.

Marquette wrote:

With a joy that I cannot express, we guided

our canoes onto the vaster eddy of the great river which I had so longed to explore.

The casual lightheartedness of the *voyageurs* diminished as they swung the canoes southward to follow the mighty course of the Mississippi River. They were highly impressed when one of their comrades, using a lead fastened to a long line, discovered that the depth of the water was 114 feet. While they were still discussing this fact, they received an unpleasant shock. Some large fish, possibly a giant catfish, cannoned against the side of Marquette's canoe with such force that the thin cedar ribs creaked and bent. This experience reduced the *voyageurs* to watchful silence for the rest of the afternoon. Fish so large were a novelty in their simple lives. That evening, after they had made camp, they used their

net in order to obtain their supper. Presently they hauled in a very deep-bodied, gray fish that had a paddle-shaped snout, oddly shaped fins, and was a good three feet in length.

Eyeing the strange shape of this creature and its large mouth with brushlike teeth, the *voyageurs*, who never had seen a paddlefish, refused to touch it. By their superstitious natures they lost themselves a good

meal, for they were unaware that a paddlefish makes particularly good eating.

"Any northern Indians would be less
fussy," Joliet said to them with a smile.
"The Father and I propose to follow their
example. We will cook that odd-looking
fish and eat it ourselves. Meanwhile, you'd
better try to catch something else."

After this experience the *voyageurs* preferred to anchor their canoes in midstream

and to sleep aboard while one of their comrades always remained awake and on watch.

The voyage went on for a week without the explorers meeting another human soul. On June 25, they discovered footprints in the mud close to the shore and a well-trodden path leading inland.

Joliet and Marquette, with considerable courage, decided to follow this trail. The sun was shining brightly, but the shade of the forest through which the path wound protected them from the great heat. They walked for six or seven miles until they saw ahead of them a stretch of open prairie. In the distance was an Indian village. It consisted of twenty or thirty tepees painted with bright colors and primitive designs. On the other side of a small river were two other villages.

"I was hoping that we might find a small party of wandering Indians," said Joliet.

"Instead of that we seem to have run into one of their main settlements. Still, it would be a pity to turn back now. I suggest we get a bit closer to them and try to form some idea as to what sort of people they are."

Joliet in his hunting costume and Marquette in his black soutane moved very cautiously through the shadowy forest until they were close enough to hear the voices of the Indians.

"They're Illinois," Marquette declared suddenly. "I met some of their tribe at my mission. They're reasonable people who will not do us any harm, and I speak their language."

They came out of the trees and began to walk boldly toward the tents. Immediately a commotion ensued among the Indians. After some delay, four elderly men walked up to the two Frenchmen, holding up befeathered calumets, or pipes of peace. All of them were wearing shirts made of French cloth. The sight of this material increased Marquette's confidence, for it showed that these Indians were almost certainly on friendly terms with French traders.

He called to them to ask who they were. As he expected, they replied saying that they were Illinois, whereupon Marquette and Joliet went forward to greet them.

As they approached the village, an old chief welcomed them from the entrance of his tent. "Frenchmen, how brightly the sun shines when you come to visit us. All our village awaits you; you shall enter our wigwams in peace."

The rest of the day was spent with these friendly people. They provided a feast for their guests. Marquette and Joliet were given bowls of Indian meal boiled with bear

fat, a large wooden platter containing fish, and other platters serving dog meat or buffalo flesh. The Frenchmen preferred to eat the buffalo.

"You may descend the great river, but you never will return," said the old chief, when Marquette began to question him.

"So we have been told," replied Marquette. "What do you think will bring about our doom?"

The chief shrugged. "It may be the great heat. If not, the ruthless tribes will kill you. Of course, you may be devoured by some of the monsters that live in the deep water. I would advise you to abandon your journey before it is too late. Stay with us here until you are rested, then return in peace and safety to your country of the north."

Buffalo robes were spread on the floor of a hut just after sunset. In spite of the latest warnings they had received, the two

Frenchmen slept peacefully throughout the night. Soon after sunrise they began their return journey to the canoes, accompanied by the chief and a large number of his warriors.

"It has been a friendly meeting," said Marquette to his companion, "but neither of us has learned a single new fact. I find it strange that all these Indians who live so close to the great river regard it with such awe and superstition."

After rejoining the *voyageurs*, who were anxiously awaiting them, Marquette and Joliet resumed their southward voyage, much to the dismay of the chief, who remained on the bank to gaze after them wistfully. That day they passed the mouth of the Illinois River and glided close to a line of jagged, strange-looking rocks on the eastern shore. They gave this place a name that was used for many years afterward by other explorers: The Ruined Castles. The *voyageurs'* confidence had returned after hearing of the friendly welcome given by the Illinois Indians. That night the whole party decided to sleep ashore.

The day was overcast and threatening when they came to the junction of the Missouri River with the Mississippi River. Under a low gray sky they saw that the tranquil surface of the river ahead of them had vanished. Instead the lumpy, swirling water was full of alarming swells and dangerous eddies. Beyond the thrusting bows of their canoes a torrent of yellow mud whirled and spouted into the deep blue current of the Mississippi. Driftwood, twisted balks of timber, and uprooted trees were being swept along by this boisterous, impatient current.

I never saw anything more terrific. This

vast torrent of water came from the northwest. I have no doubt that it may provide a route to another ocean. I believe that this other ocean is the Vermilion Sea (Gulf of California).

Marquette's enormous interest in exploration prompted him to end this page in his journal with the words: "I hope someday to be able to follow this inviting channel."

About this time Marquette began to feel the first signs of approaching illness. He had inherited the robust constitution of his French fellow-countrymen, but for years he had devoted himself to study and paid little attention to his health. During the merciless cold of Canadian winters he had nourished himself with poor and inadequate food. His strength was beginning to diminish and his body's resistance to the hardships of a primitive way of life had become insufficient.

Marquette was the only member of the expedition to suffer from ill health. Joliet and his *voyageurs* were reveling in the increasing warmth of the weather and the unfailing supplies of fresh meat and fish. They remained ignorant for a long time of the fact that their amiable companion, Father Marquette, was beginning to suffer from an abdominal complaint called dysentery. Marquette preferred to keep the matter a secret for as long as he could.

Next they came to the mouth of the Ohio River, as it was named by the Iroquois. The forests were thinning out now and so were the outcrops of rock and crag that the explorers had passed frequently during the earlier stages of their voyage. The shores were becoming low and marshy. Instead of oak and walnut and maple, the warm breeze filtered through dense growths of straight-stemmed, feathery-headed cane.

The noonday sun was becoming so intense that the *voyageurs* had given up paddling except in the cool hours of dawn and the late afternoon. The canoes were equipped with small canvas sails. The men used these sails to contrive a kind of awning under which they rested during the midday hours while the friendly current continued to sweep them along.

Early in July the Frenchmen suddenly caught sight of some Chickasaw Indians on the swampy eastern shore. The canoes were noticed at the same moment. The Indians began to yell excitedly. They rushed to their huts and reappeared with bows and spears. The Frenchmen replied by reaching for their muskets, which always lay loaded beside the thwarts. Marquette immediately raised aloft the calumet given him by the Illinois. When the Indians saw this symbol of peace, they lowered their weapons and

61

made signs to the explorers to paddle toward the shore.

One or two of these Indians carried muskets. Several others were armed with steel knives and axes. Their language was unknown, but they indicated by signs that they had obtained these articles from English traders who lived far to the east. Later in the day their leader appeared and began to speak the Illinois tongue well enough for Marquette to understand.

"I have heard of you French people of the far North," said this leader. "The English have told us that you and your countrymen are few in numbers, that your trade goods are of poor quality, and that one day they will drive you all into the sea. All these things may be true, but you have not been afraid to come far down this river. Never yet have I seen one of the English venturing along its shores. I begin to wonder if they are not perhaps afraid to come across the (Appalachian) mountains."

The Frenchmen were given a meal of "buffalo meat, bear's oil, and white plums." In reply to a question put to him by Joliet, the chief gave the inaccurate information that the mouth of the river could be reached in another ten days of paddling. We know today that the Frenchmen were in what is now the State of Tennessee and still many hundreds of miles to the north of the Mississippi delta.

Joliet himself was a little doubtful of the Indian's estimate of distance, but the other Frenchmen felt somewhat encouraged by the news. They continued to float downstream past lonely and apparently uninhabited shores, which consisted almost entirely, as Marquette said, "of river, marsh and forest."

They were nearing the mouth of the Arkansas River when they sighted a cluster of wigwams on the western bank. The Indian occupants rushed down to the water's edge and, with much yelling and brandishing of weapons, launched their own heavy wooden canoes, some of which held eight to ten men. While some of the Indians hastily prepared their weapons, their companions paddled swiftly into midstream so as to cut off the canoes from flight in any direction. A man in the nearest canoe hurled his tomahawk, which sailed above the Frenchmen's heads.

Jacques, the *voyageur*, aimed his musket at the fellow, but Joliet ordered him not to fire. Marquette, who was seated amidships, was still holding up the Illinois calumet. Some of the older men who had remained on the bank saw this pipe of peace and shouted angrily at the young men in the canoes. The latter glanced toward the shore and then lowered their weapons. An elderly man, who appeared to be the chief, made signs to the French to approach.

Shaken and trembling, they stepped onto the beach. They found a better reception than they had expected. The chief spoke a little of the Illinois tongue and listened to the account that Marquette gave him.

"Yours is the greatest canoe voyage I have heard of," the chief said admiringly.

He repeated the story to the clustered villagers, who quickly became gay, civil, and lighthearted. They laid aside their spears and bows to take part in the feast that followed. Marquette and the others slept in the village that night.

"You will be safe if you go on down this river for another day's journey," said this Arkansas chief. "Beyond that distance, you will be risking your lives with every stroke of your paddles. The tribes who live farther downstream are our enemies. They are armed with guns they have obtained from the white men. Being proud of these weapons, they like to shoot every stranger who enters their country. Sometimes they kill themselves instead, for they load their guns with much powder and the barrel bursts."

The chief paused and glanced thoughtfully at Marquette and his companions. "I am sure that other tribes up the river have told you many strange tales of the dangers that await you," he said shrewdly. "This time you are hearing the truth. Go more than a day's journey downstream, and you will lose your lives."

Joliet discussed this news while they lay in their hut that night. "The chief seems very well informed," said Joliet. "I believe that the downstream Indians really are different, as he said. Do you remember that he described them as living in large, square buildings built of sunbaked bricks mixed with straw and covered with dome-shaped roofs of straw? Everything about them seems strange to me, and I very much doubt if we could talk to them in any of the Indian languages that we know."

"Let us go on at least to the next village," Marquette suggested. "If they confirm what the chief of this village has said, then I think we should go no farther."

They embarked in their canoes next morning at sunrise. After paddling most of the day they reached the village, which was twenty-five miles away. In some strange way the Taensas Indians of this village already had learned of their approach and were awaiting the Frenchmen on the bank of the river.

Once again Joliet and his companions were entertained generously and fed on roasted dog, fish, buffalo meat, and porridge

made of Indian meal. One of the young
warriors spoke a little of the Illinois language, and he made the meaning of his
words even clearer by the use of vivid signs.

Speaking on behalf of his chief, he said,
"Do not go on down this river, the mouth
of which lies 500 miles (it was actually 700
miles) farther on. If you are not killed by
the treacherous Quinipassas Indians, you
may be captured by the men of a white race

who are extremely cruel and suspicious of everyone. I have seen some of them. When they speak together, their language does not sound like your own."

Clearly the young Indian was referring to the Spaniards, and this information worried Joliet even more. Both Marquette and he knew how jealous the Spaniards were of any other European who ventured into the tempting waters of the Mexican Gulf. At that time Spain looked upon the whole Caribbean Sea and the countries adjacent to it as a valuable possession of her own empire. Hanging, imprisonment, or slavery was the usual fate reserved for unfortunate strangers.

"I think we have gone far enough to help the geographers," said Marquette. "In past years they have argued whether this river discharges into the Atlantic Ocean or into the Gulf of California. We have taken regular compass bearings throughout our voyage. Now we can say with confidence that this river flows into the Gulf of Mexico."

"And if we risk our lives at this stage, all the information we have gathered may be lost to France," added Joliet. "As the leader of this expedition I am responsible for our safety. In any case, I doubt if I could persuade our *voyageurs* to continue much farther. They are beginning to understand what the Indians say, and they would not be happy at the thought of running into the Spanish. They are homesick for New France, and I must confess I share their feelings."

Marquette and Joliet then had reached a location slightly to the north of the future site of the Mississippi town of Greenville. On July 17, 1673, they re-embarked in their canoes and turned their faces to the north. During that first day of the return journey the *voyageurs* indicated their relief by frequently bursting into song.

Paddling upstream against the current in the great heat of midsummer was exhausting. The *voyageurs* were young and sturdy men, but their lives had been spent in the colder climate and fresher winds of New France. Hours of monotonous toil at the paddles left them sweating and tired by the end of the day. Joliet, a young man of unusual strength and endurance, took his share of the paddling, and he, too, was weary by the time that evening came. Nor was poor Father Marquette able to give the cheerful assistance he had rendered during the southward voyage. He had been forced to reveal his increasing illness to his companions. Now he was obliged to spend much of his time on a buffalo robe in the bottom of his canoe.

When at last they reached the mouth of the Illinois River, a party of Indians gave Joliet a helpful suggestion.

"If you take your canoes up this river," they said, "you will reach the southern end of Lake Michigan more quickly. It is a much shorter route than the one you came down by."

Joliet took their advice. He was anxious

74

for the voyage to end as quickly as possible so that Father Marquette could have more rest and better attention.

The Illinois River made a pleasant change after the wide and monotonous surface of the Mississippi. The current flowed less strongly, innumerable groves of shade-providing trees afforded ideal campsites, and the rich green valleys between the friendly hills were covered with grazing herds of deer and bison. The glare and stagnant heat of the great river had been left behind. Although the sun continued its daily course across a cloudless sky, the breeze held a tang of welcome freshness that spoke to the *voyageurs* of home, and the starlit nights were cool and clear.

The canoes reached Lake Michigan and coasted northward along its western shore. At the end of September the Frenchmen were back among their old friends, the

Wild Oats Indians of Green Bay. They had been absent for about four months and during that time they had voyaged more than 2500 miles.

Joliet was not in a mood to waste time in this friendly area. He and his men paddled on to the mission post at Michilimackinac as swiftly as possible. Marquette was placed on a comfortable couch, and two other Jesuit fathers were found to care for him. Joliet himself also remained at the mission until the early spring of 1674.

He explained his stopover to Marquette by saying that he wished to complete his journal of the voyage and to check certain passages in it with the journal kept by Marquette himself. But Joliet's true reason was to help the Jesuit fathers care for his companion.

"They are already hard put to care for their converts and to look after themselves," he said to Marquette. "In addition, they are not allowed to use a musket to hunt for fresh meat. But I have some slight skill with medicinal herbs, and as long as we remain here you will not go without the rich broths and meats your body needs."

Marquette was grateful but worried. He had heard enough of Count Frontenac to know that the imperious new governor-general would want a report on the trip right away. Also, Marquette's education enabled him to realize perhaps more fully than Joliet of what tremendous importance to New France their discovery of the course of the Mississippi River might be. Thus, in the spring of 1674, when Marquette's condition had improved considerably, he urged his companion to set off for Quebec without wasting more time.

"Your canoe man, Pierre, has agreed to remain with me," said Marquette. "He is a handy fellow and skilled with his cooking pot. You, Joliet, must leave at once, for the ice is melting and the waterways will be open. Good fortune go with you, my friend, and I shall pray that we may meet again."

The good fortune that had guarded Joliet during his long trip down the Mississippi River suddenly abandoned him almost entirely. In the wide and leaping waters of the vast Lachine Rapids just below Montreal, his canoe was upset. Two of his *voyageurs* and an Indian boy who was with them were drowned in the muddy floodwaters. All Joliet's papers, including his maps and report, were lost. Joliet himself managed to struggle ashore with the two surviving *voyageurs*. Their canoe was lost forever.

Joliet wrote to Frontenac:

I had escaped every peril from the Indians.

I had passed forty-two rapids and was on the point of disembarking, full of joy at the success of so long and difficult an enterprise, when my canoe capsized after all the danger seemed over. I lost two men and my box of papers within sight of the first French settlements which I had left more than a year before.

Joliet remained in Quebec to rewrite his journal from memory as best he could. Meanwhile, Marquette spent his convalescence completing his own journal of the voyage and sent it to the Jesuit Mission in Quebec a few months after Joliet had left him. The arrival of his report enabled Joliet to carry out his own task. While Marquette's report was passed on by the Jesuits to their superiors in Paris, Joliet's was submitted to Frontenac, who, after reading it, submitted the journal to the king.

By the autumn of 1674, Marquette felt

strong enough to resume his missionary duties. His memories of the great river and its friendly tribes had remained with him during his months of illness. During the summer of 1674, while he was still far from well, he had written to the Father Superior in Quebec for permission to establish a mission in the chief village of the Illinois tribe.

His request was approved. On October 25, he set off with Pierre and another Frenchman. A number of Illinois Indians went with them.

The little fleet reached the southern shore of Lake Michigan at the end of November. The bright greenery of the forest was darkening and turning to a rusty brown with the approach of winter. Marquette landed on the future site of Chicago, through which he had passed already on his northward journey with Joliet. His old illness returned at that stage, and he became unable to continue the southward journey.

His two French companions discussed what they should do. "We cannot risk a winter journey back to the mission," they decided. "The Father would never survive it. Let us build a good cabin here, where he will be able to rest in warmth and comfort throughout the winter."

Six miles inland from the southern shore of Lake Michigan, they and their Indian helpers quickly erected a log-walled cabin. Buffalo and deer roamed the area, and wild turkeys were abundant. Passing friendly Indians supplied them with corn. Two French *coureurs de bois*, who also were camping nearby, came often to see Marquette and did what little they could to raise his spirits.

In March, 1675, Marquette had recovered somewhat. The two Frenchmen urged him to return to Michilimackinac, but he insisted on continuing his journey to the Illinois. The little flotilla of canoes containing Indians and Frenchmen glided down the swollen waters of the Des Plaines River, past gray, saturated prairies and forests that winter had stripped of foliage.

They reached the Illinois River and embarked on its surface. Six days later they reached the main village of the Illinois tribe, a place called Kaskaskia. At this time the village contained about seventy-four lodges, each of which contained several families. (This village was about seven miles south of the modern Illinois town of Ottawa.)

The Indians gave Marquette a friendly welcome, but Pierre and his companion became more worried with every day that passed. Father Marquette's health and strength were decreasing rapidly, yet he still refused to take all the rest he needed.

Pierre was the one who finally insisted. "We are going to take you back to Michilimackinac," he said bluntly. "If you remain here, your illness never will be cured. This is no place in which to endure a long sickness and to risk even death."

Marquette finally agreed. His two loyal friends took him back to Michigan. Many of the Illinois came with them to give what assistance they could. The sick missionary was placed on buffalo robes in the bottom of the roomy canoe. The two Frenchmen then set out on the long journey up the lake. Spring had come to New France, and the voyage was made in sunny and favorable weather, but Marquette continued to grow weaker.

On May 19, 1675, he asked his companions to make for the shore. There they built a small hut. As they placed him on a rough couch, he murmured, "I thank God that I

am about to die in the wilderness, a missionary of the Faith and a member of the
Jesuit brotherhood."

In the cold, bright dawn of the following
day, Marquette rallied for a few brief moments. To Pierre he said, "I pray you to
convey my greetings and last farewell to my
friend Joliet, with whom I shared a great
adventure and through whose kindness I
made a voyage of which I often had

dreamed. May my blessings go with him on the trails and waterways he will follow in years to come."

Father Jacques Marquette was buried beside the little bark shelter in which he had spent his last night. Pierre and his companion then paddled on to the mission of Saint Ignace at Michilimackinac, where they reported the news.

Joliet remained in ignorance of Marquette's death until September in that year of 1675. He was in Quebec when the faithful Pierre, in baggy homespun coat, knee breeches, woolen stockings, and soft leather shoes, came in search of him.

"He was a man of God," Pierre said bluntly, "but he could have been a man like you, and he was your true friend, *monsieur*."

"Father Marquette was one of the few friends, apart from you my *voyageurs*, that

I have had in the wilderness," Joliet replied sadly. "Once I tried to be a priest, and when I failed I became an explorer. Father Marquette was a great missionary, but he proved that he could have been a great explorer too."

The life of Louis Joliet continued to be eventful. On October 7, 1675, Joliet married Claire Bissot, the daughter of a wealthy fur merchant who was engaged in trade with the northern Indians. No sooner was he married than Joliet, who had never seen the territory to the north, decided to make his way up there. He ascended the Saguenay River with a couple of his hardy *voyageurs*, one of whom was the faithful Pierre. Then, leaving the river, they struck off on foot across muskeg country until they reached the Rupert River and followed it to the shores of Hudson's Bay.

Joliet sighted three English forts on the edge of the Bay, each of which was held by a small but strongly armed garrison. Cruising the icy and lonely waters of the Bay itself was a broad-beamed and waddling little trading vessel armed with twelve guns.

Englishmen of any kind were much more reassuring to Joliet than some of the Indians he had met on his travels. Thus, he marched up to the nearest fort, informed the occupants who he was, and — while having a friendly drink with them — said bluntly how sorry he was to find them there. Hudson's Bay, he said firmly, rightfully belonged to New France.

The English appreciated his frankness and his enormous knowledge of the vast country that lay to the south. They invited him into their forts and entertained him to hearty meals.

"Why not join us?" they asked one night,

while they were eating and drinking together. "We would have great use for a man like you, who has so much experience as an explorer and knows the Indians so well. You would earn more money with us than you'll ever get by risking your neck as a French fur trader."

"I like my independence even better than your good English gold," Joliet replied. "And I must say that I sooner would help my fellow-countrymen to remove you from this territory than assist you to settle yourselves more firmly along its shores."

The Englishmen laughed. They found most Frenchmen difficult to deal with, but with Joliet they always knew where they stood. When he set off on his return voyage, they saw that his canoe was well laden with excellent provisions.

Joliet returned to Quebec where he reported to the French authorities that unless they expelled the English, the northern fur trade would be lost to New France forever. The officials made only a few tepid moves to act on Joliet's warning, but they handed him a generous reward for what he had done. He was given the great island of Anticosti lying at the mouth of the Saint Lawrence River. Living on this island, which measures 140 miles by 28 miles and is a game preserve today, he kept his cherished independence and established a profitable fishery. In his spare time he made considerable use of his skill as a navigator and surveyor to prepare an excellent chart of the Saint Lawrence River. During his absences from Anticosti, the fishery was managed by his wife and her mother, who was now a widow.

For ten or eleven years life passed peacefully for Joliet and his family. Then misfortune came to them in 1690 when Sir William Phips, who was a lusty adventurer with a touch of the buccaneer, arrived off Anticosti with a ramshackle fleet of New England ships. Sir William was on his way to attack Quebec in response to French attacks on New England. However, he stayed at the island to burn Joliet's fishery and to take his wife and mother-in-law prisoner. Joliet, who was away at the time, escaped capture. The New Englanders then sailed on up the river, where they received a tremendous hammering from the heavy guns mounted on the Citadel of Quebec. Sir William and his fleet retreated down the Saint Lawrence, pausing long enough at Anticosti to set ashore Claire Joliet and her tough, outspoken mother. They were probably glad to be rid of these two angry and fearless women. Joliet himself had arrived at the island in the meantime and was on hand for the return of his wife and mother-in-law.

Joliet then rebuilt his fishery. Four years later he set off to explore the coast of Labrador as a possible area for a whale and seal fishery. On his return, Governor Frontenac — who approved of daring characters as long as they kept out of politics — appointed him royal pilot for the Saint Lawrence.

Joliet held this rank until he died in the year 1699. At his own request, he was buried on one of the lonely Mingan islands in that same great river. Like his friend Marquette, Joliet always preferred the unspoiled wilderness and chose it for his final resting place.

The reports written by Marquette and Joliet might have been left to gather dust in the royal library of the royal Palace of Versailles. But Robert La Salle, the daring and imaginative explorer, came to hear of them and studied them eagerly. His interest was increased by the fact that he had met Joliet, who was a man of about his own age.

The descriptions of the Mississippi River stirred La Salle's imaginative ambition, and he set off to explore it in 1682. Accompanied by six canoes containing Frenchmen and Indians, he voyaged down the Mississippi, reached its mouth, and claimed the country for France. Upon the whole beautiful region he bestowed the name of Louisiana. Such was the first great result of the humble but important voyage made by Marquette and Joliet.

The actual area now claimed by France included the fertile plains of Texas and the vast basin of the Mississippi River. The French moved into the region and soon began to multiply and prosper, while their white-walled farms rose along the banks of the great river. Near the southern end of the Mississippi, the fortified settlement of New Orleans was founded in 1717.

Some of those lonely settlements and trading posts grew into the great modern cities of today. Among them are Saint Louis, Minneapolis, Milwaukee, Biloxi, Baton Rouge, and Kansas City. Each was founded by the hardy French traders and farmers who followed in the wake of Marquette and Joliet.

France's ownership of this enormous region ended in 1803, when President Jefferson purchased the whole of Louisiana for a total payment of $15 million. Nine years later, in 1812, Louisiana became a state of the Union. Even today, however, the shadows of Marquette, Joliet, and La Salle still overhang much of Louisiana. Throughout the area French names and customs remain in use and set the region apart from the rest of the United States.

Bibliography

Burpee, Lawrence, J. *Discovery of Canada.* Toronto: The Macmillan Company of Canada Limited, 1946

Parkman, Francis. *Count Frontenac and New France.* London: Macmillan and Company Limited, 1885

Parkman, Francis. *La Salle and the Discovery of the Great West.* Boston: Little, Brown and Company, 1903

Parkman, Francis. *The Struggle for a Continent.* London: Macmillan and Company Limited, 1902

Winsor, Justin. *From Cartier to Frontenac: Geographical Discovery in the Interior of North America in Its Historical Relations 1534–1700.* New York: Cooper Square Publishers, Inc., 1970

75-607

920
SYM

Syme, Ronald

Marquette and
Joliet: voyagers
on the Mississippi